We were all on this ship in the sixties, our generation, a ship going to discover the New World. And the Beatles were in the crow's nest of that ship.

John Lennon

I think maybe people see bands and musicians as some sort of superhero unrealistic sport that happens in another dimension where it's not real people and not real emotions. So, I grew up listening to Beatles records on my floor. That's how I learned how to play guitar. If it weren't for them, I wouldn't be a musician.

Dave Grohl

It was my love for the guitar that first got me into music and singing. Growing up, I was inspired by The Beatles and Bob Dylan. Damian Rice was a huge influence for me musically.

Ed Sheeran

With the Beatles, we'd been very spoiled because we had George Martin who worked for the record label we were going to be signed to. That was very fortunate, because we grew together.

Paul McCartney

India brings out so many different feelings in me. I've been fascinated with India and Indian culture as long as I can remember - ever since the '60s with the Beatles and Maharishi Mahesh Yogi.

Joe Perry

I did not break up the Beatles. You can't have it both ways. If you're going to blame me for breaking the Beatles up, you should be thankful that I made them into myth rather than a crumbling group.

Yoko Ono

People don't realize what they had till it's gone. Like President Kennedy, there was no one like him, the Beatles, and my man Elvis Presley. I was the Elvis of boxing.

Muhammad Ali

You have to be a bastard to make it, and that's a fact. And the Beatles are the biggest bastards on earth.

John Lennon

From one generation to the next, The Beatles will remain the most important rock band of all time.

Dave Grohl

Somebody said to me, 'But the Beatles were anti-materialistic.' That's a huge myth. John and I literally used to sit down and say, 'Now, let's write a swimming pool.'

Paul McCartney

As far as I'm concerned, there won't be a Beatles reunion as long as John Lennon remains dead.

George Harrison

There are only four people who knew what the Beatles were about anyway.

Paul McCartney

I went from being a kid-kid, listen to everything from The Beatles through Kiss, Peter Frampton, Jethro Tull classic rock, classic stuff into immediately, it seemed like, Iron Maiden and stuff like that. The first Iron Maiden record and then, obviously, the first Metallica record.

Phil Anselmo

Downloadable music is the biggest musical phenomenon since the Beatles, and the music industry is slow to come to grips with that.

Chuck D

The artist that had the biggest impact on me was Michael Jackson. He was my Elvis and Beatles. When I was 15, I listened to a lot of Sinatra, but my jean jacket didn't have, 'I love Frank' on it, it had, 'I love AC/DC', 'Guns N Roses', 'Pearl Jam'. I thought Eddie Vedder was the second coming.

Michael Buble

The Beatles saved the world from boredom.

George Harrison

The Beatles created something that never trailed off. What a gift that was to their fans. If you're into the Beatles, you loved them from beginning to end.

Jerry Seinfeld

When you think about rock at its origin, and you think of the Beatles and millions of kids screaming as loud as they can and running as fast as they can towards the Beatles, there's no one who is that kind of lightning rod, who commands that kind of power and has that kind of creative magma.

Jack Black

The Beatles will exist without us.

George Harrison

The Beatles will go on and on.

George Harrison

Being in The Beatles was a short, incredible period of my life. I had 22 years leading up to it, and it was all over eight years later.

Ringo Starr

I like What Goes Around Comes Around for old concert tees. Oh man, I got this 'Sgt. Pepper' cartoon Beatles shirt there; it was, like, $300. I didn't even know how much it cost - I thought it was gonna be, like, $80 at most - till I got to the register and was like, 'Oh mah gawd!' Good Lord. But it's classic vintage rock, you know?

Kid Cudi

In Malaysia, where Western culture was extremely influential, I'd grown up listening to Elvis and the Beatles and watching American movies. People wanted to be like Americans. In contrast, when I got here, I saw prosperous middle-class American college students wanting to somehow join the Third World.

Feisal Abdul Rauf

The biggest break in my career was getting into the Beatles in 1962. The second biggest break since then is getting out of them.

George Harrison

I am a big Beatles fan. And, you know, unbeknownst to anyone, I used to be one. But I have no problems of putting titles and lines from other songs in my songs, because they're great lines and great titles.

Ringo Starr

I don't relate to the 'Twilight' books or movies at all, but I'm obsessed with it as a pop culture phenomenon - all these people just screaming like it was the Beatles.

Lykke Li

While other girls swooned over The Beatles and the Rolling Stones, I worshipped Rudolf Nureyev and Isadora Duncan.

Celia Imrie

I'm touched by rock n' roll. I'm touched by the Beatles. I want some of the music I do to reflect that.

Al Jarreau

We were very influenced by The Beatles, no question.

Barry Gibb

I love the Beatles. I haven't named any kids after them but I still really love them. They were the first group that I was ever properly aware of. In my early teens I would sometimes stay in and listen to the radio all day in the hope that I would catch a song by them that I'd never heard before and be able to tape it on my radio-cassette player.

Jarvis Cocker

By 1968, both The Beatles and The Beach Boys had plenty of fame - we were looking for something deeper. The Maharishi taught us how to go beyond thinking and action in order to grow from within.

Mike Love

In the spring of 1968, The Beatles and I were invited by Maharishi Mahesh Yogi to travel to Riskikesh, India. Riskikesh has been an important spiritual place to many millions of people over the years. It is situated where the Ganges River flows out of the Himalayas, and to be in that atmosphere was something incredibly special.

Mike Love

People say the Beatles were John Lennon. What is Paul McCartney? Chopped liver? But everyone has their own favourite members whose creativity they gravitate to. That's normal.

Mike Love

We came from the '60s era, when we started and made so many hits. The song value from the '60s was so darn good, you've got The Beatles, The Beach Boys, all of Motown, and plenty of other people, too... amazing records, amazing songs.

Mike Love

The Beatles, the Small Faces and the Kinks were great bands, but that was in the '60s.

Gavin Rossdale

The Beatles did their best cover work on Little Richard's 'Long Tall Sally' and music influenced by Richard, such as Larry Williams's 'Dizzy Miss Lizzie.'

Jon Landau

When the Beatles cut old rock n' roll, they were recording music still in their performing repertoire, and besides, they never thought of the music as old.

Jon Landau

My parents met in music school and my father was a music professor and conductor. Growing up, we always had classical and contemporary music playing. There was a lot of Mozart and the Beatles.

Sara Zarr

The Beatles had just come out, and everybody had a band. It was incredible competition out there.

Gregg Allman

Even the Beatles found it hard to escape their image; they were trapped by it.

Tina Weymouth

Obviously the people that I admired, like the Beatles, were really into rock'n'roll, but it was already a little past rock'n'roll when I started listening and making my own choices about music.

Elvis Costello

My first favorite band that made music important to me was the Beatles. I was a little kid. I didn't know who was singing what song or who wrote what song.

Chris Cornell

The '60s in London obviously brought about the explosion of music, the 'Beatles' especially, and then the 'Rolling Stones' and other forms of music, and then fashion and photography and films - kitchen-sink dramas we called them at that time, which was our 'nouvelle vague' in Britain, films that talk about real life.

Charlotte Rampling

I don't care if it's rap, metal, whatever. You still should play Beatles records mixed with Limp Bizkit mixed with Foghat mixed with Creedence Clearwater Revival, stuff like that.

Afrika Bambaataa

Everyone's seen the Beatles.

Dhani Harrison

I've been playing my instrument since I was about three or four. That's when I started banging around on the piano, trying to be like The Beatles.

Nat Wolff

If you want to be negative about the whole thing you can say all guitar bands after the Beatles were just a waste of time because the Beatles were the best. I think it's far better to give new records a try.

Stephen Malkmus

I just found out last week - my sister told me - that my father had some Beatles records. So I must have heard them quite a bit, but it never registered, really. Now I listen to them with new ears.

Sheryl Lee

I like the Beatles, of course, but that's when I grew up.

Elizabeth Moon

Stevie Wonder doing 'We Can Work It Out' by the Beatles is one of my favorite records of all time.

Mark Ronson

Danny and I wrote 10 songs in seven days, which I thought might be close to the record until you probably look at some of the Beatles statistics.

Jerry Only

The Beatles mean so much to so many people, you know? Everybody has at least one song of The Beatles that's one of their favorite songs of all time.

Evan Rachel Wood

Before the Beatles, songwriters were very anonymous people and nobody paid any attention to them.

Bjorn Ulvaeus

I know when I started I would have been happy to sound like the Beatles or Joe Tex or whoever. You want to sound like most bands, you want to sound like their records and that's how you learn your chops.

Jon Anderson

I met The Beatles and Stones at the same time, because Michael Cooper was doing several of their album covers.

Terry Southern

Probably my two biggest musical influences were the Everly Brothers and the Beatles, in chronological order. Both of them have had a very simple-sounding musical style that's actually quite complex as far as popular songs are concerned.

Arlo Guthrie

I would sell 2 million records, a million went to teenagers and a million went to the adults. So, when The Beatles became so popular, I lost a million to the teenagers, but I was still selling a million to the adults.

Bobby Vinton

Like all teenagers in the early '60s, I put down my hockey stick when the Beatles got big and picked up a guitar. We all thought we'd be rock stars. Then I got into comedy, but I'd always find a way to use my guitar, such as writing songs and doing musical parodies.

Rick Moranis

When the Beatles hit in the early '60s, I think the objection was more to the hair than the music. The McCartney melodies were undeniably beautiful. The parents of my generation couldn't deny 'Yesterday.' I happen to have been partial to the Beatles, but a lot of kids loved the Rolling Stones, and I don't know what their parents thought of them.

Rick Moranis

It was an experience being on a Beatles tour. They weren't very good. The singing was great, but the playing was a bit weak.

Robin Trower

I just got exposed to electronica, and I really liked it. I am also good with alternative rock. I like Lana Del Rey, Adele, Dido, Jack Johnson, and I love the Beatles and the Beach Boys.

Anushka Sharma

One of my favorite albums is Bob Gibson and Bob Camp, 'At the Gate of Horn.' It was a really dynamic album, almost like The Beatles, and way before its time... around 1960 or so.

Roger McGuinn

Maybe 'Can't Stop Feeling' and 'Turn It On' we'll just release as singles. It's a thing The Beatles used to do which I really loved, the idea of releasing something as a single completely on its own.

Alex Kapranos

People have made a living deconstructing Lennon and The Beatles songs because of their compositional sophistication. But what's so exciting about John is that he never had any of that training on musical theory; something just spoke to him, and he just knew what sounded right.

Randy Bachman

Like any family, like any group - the Beatles, Led Zeppelin, EPMD, Public Enemy - they've had bumps in the road. I just think that because A Tribe Called Quest is so precious to fans, they were concerned about unveiling some of those things.

Michael Rapaport

I mean, Beatles songs were two and a half minutes long, and they're fantastic.

Billy Sherwood

I liked a lot of the things other people liked - Jimi Hendrix, The Beatles, Van Halen, AC/DC - but if I compared it to my dad's music, there just seemed to be elements missing.

Dweezil Zappa

One of my main problems with music is that the basic formula is always the same: verse, chorus, verse, chorus, bridge, verse, chorus, chorus, chorus, end. One of the bands that changed that was The Beatles. If you listen to 'Everybody's Got Something to Hide Except Me and My Monkey.' It's three verses, bridge, end.

Buzz Osborne

I think great songs appeal to people at any age. Kids love the Beatles, too. Kids love Tom T. Hall. Of course, Tom T. wrote some things that were specifically for kids. But I think kids recognize quality more than they get credit for sometimes.

Jason Isbell

I thought if Oasis could get away with sounding like The Beatles, I could get away with sounding like Abba.

Pete Waterman

My dad is a huge folk music fan, so growing up, there were always records playing in my house. Carole King, James Taylor, Simon and Garfunkel, the Beatles - I grew up with this music, and I was aware of how special this music was to a lot of people.

Jake Epstein

It's funny, because in 1970 I met the Beatles quite by a chance at a party. It was the Beethoven bicentenary, and I was then also playing the Beethoven Sonatas. And that's all they wanted to hear about - I wanted to talk about them, and all they wanted to talk about was Beethoven.

Daniel Barenboim

I was so busy with my studies that I didn't have a musical idol as a teenager. Later, around my 20s, I suddenly discovered the Beatles and the Rolling Stones but I guess my musical idol has always been Strauss.

Andre Rieu

I learned to play piano in a rock n' roll context or band context from country records - you know, Floyd Cramer - and from the Beatles and the Rolling Stones and Stax. And none of those are keyboard records.

Benmont Tench

Listen to the Beatles' 'Things We Said Today.' Ringo Starr does not play a fill in the entire song. It doesn't need it. 'A Day In the Life' has gorgeous fills, but there, the song needs it. When I play on any record, I'm striving to get where Ringo is. You play what doesn't take you out of the song.

Benmont Tench

We listened to a lot of Rolling Stones and Beatles records when we were recording. They were really good at not playing loud, but generating really big sounds out of everything.

Mike Lowry

Funny songs aren't usually that good. Like Weird Al and maybe a couple of Beatles songs, but it's kind of hard to bring humor into rock music in an interesting way.

Win Butler

They said hey look, The Beatles deserve to be number one, not Bobby Vinton. We're gonna cut your tires. Change that listing. They were dedicated at the time.

Bobby Vinton

The Dave Clark Five had more appearances on 'The Ed Sullivan Show' than The Beatles.

Paul Shaffer

When I was a tiny tot, we only had one record player in the house, so there was either Genesis on it or the Jungle Book or The Beatles as well, and various other things.

Rick Astley

Everybody can dig The Beatles, but why should everybody dig us?

Bruce Johnston

For us... you know, we're not The Beatles.

Bruce Johnston

Cole Archer's Chillout Mix. That's my son's mix. He's ten weeks old, and this is what he listens to: 'Valerie' by Amy Winehouse, 'Everyday People' by Arrested Development, The

Beatles' 'Rocky Raccoon,' and Bruce Springsteen's 'Atlantic City.'

Adam Pally

I grew up listening to pop; I grew up listening to '60s pop music, the Beatles, the Monkees, Herman's Hermits and all that stuff. So I had a very strong background of listening to great pop music.

Jane Wiedlin

I was 16 when I started playing. I borrowed a friend's acoustic guitar, and I had a Beatles chord book. I just taught myself that way.

Britt Daniel

I remembered their songs but I had never owned a Beatles album.

Sheryl Lee

My roots are more in he Beatles, Zeppelin, the whole 60's side.

Pat Mastelotto

If I could be in any band, I think it would have to be The Beatles. That would have been a lot of fun.

Jason Behr

I heard the Beatles and the Stones, and Mom bought me an electric guitar. I played lead for four years and then switched to bass. One day someone suggested that I should sing, so I sheepishly stepped up to the microphone and the rest is rock history.

Glenn Hughes

I heard Q-Tip on the Jungle Brothers' song 'The Promo.' It was very exciting. It was very new. The music and the culture around hip-hop was evolving. I think there's an emotional quality to their music and there's a vulnerability to the music. For me, A Tribe Called Quest was my Beatles.

Michael Rapaport

So to compare the Beatles, obviously the Beatles are the Beatles, but in hip-hop terms, Tribe is the Beatles. Grandmaster Flash and the Furious Five are the Beatles. Big Daddy Kane is Jimi Hendrix. It means that much to people that grew up with it.

Michael Rapaport

The music I listened to as a kid - the Stones, the Beatles - that was so rebellious at the time, it became mainstream.

Ian Schrager

A lost of people recognize me and maybe will ask for an autograph, but it's nothing like if Elvis would've done something like that, 'cause he's so popular, or maybe The Beatles 'cause they stirred up a lot of action.

Mickey Gilley

When I first started making music, it was learning other people's songs and putting them onto four-track. Like Beatles songs and stuff. When I started writing, I used the singing side of the production as a vehicle for melody and lyrical ideas.

M. Ward

I play guitar and I love the Beatles and melodic music.

Stephen Dorff

I grew up listening to most of my parents' music like The Beatles and ABBA and all that stuff.

Tammin Sursok

I wouldn't know how I would have coped with The Beatles' sort of fame.

Noel Redding

It's in the vein, somewhere in a cross between The Beatles, Cheap Trick, The Stones, Badfinger, you know, but it's not retro at all. But it is very pop.

Steve Brown

I wish I lived in the '60s because I'm a big fan of the Beatles.

Celine Buckens

Some people have been listening to the Beatles their whole lives; I didn't discover them until I was 18 years old.

Danger Mouse

He made it quite clear that if I didn't play the role, I would be dead within a week. As you can imagine, the guy who turned down Hagrid would be like the guy who called the Beatles a guitar band. So I couldn't possibly refuse, really.

Robbie Coltraine

It's marvelous when you visit Tokyo: they have these clubs, and they'll have 'Motown Night' or 'The Beatles - Totally Authentic and Live!' You know it's shrunk, but at least there's some sort of youthful figure to it. Whereas, the blues scene in Europe is more like, 'Here we go again.'

Robert Palmer

But times changed, and I changed, and I didn't feel that way anymore. The Beatles were happening. I think that was probably the main thing. The Beatles just changed the whole world of music.

Barry McGuire

I was lucky enough to see the Beatles play live.

Jon English

The best pop music is the songs that a group of people can dance to, but you can also listen to in your bed and cry. That's something obviously that The Beatles started and... so having that darkness there opens another door.

Jack Antonoff

The awesomeness of God is that even in the works of the Beach Boys, Beatles, etc., the beauty of the music is a mere reflection of what God does everyday. He creates music of all kinds and moods.

John Foster

Because when the film was first mooted, the Beatles didn't like the idea at all. In fact they wouldn't have any part in it. And when Brian had committed them, it was part of a deal he did with United Artists, I think.

George Martin

My dad was in a Beatles cover band. My mom wore Candies and belly buttons. The people in our family were very glamorous. They wore pearls like Jackie O.

Azita Ghanizada

Growing up, I put a lot of pressure on myself. I felt with The Beatles legacy that there was pressure on me to do music, and while I always loved music and it was always around me at home, I thought about doing other things.

James McCartney

The first year with the success that we had and let me point out that the time frame changes depending on which decade you look at it. In the seventies acts were kind of expected to do an album a year. If you look at the Beatles they were doing three a year.

Gerry Beckley

When I first started playing in a band, before the Beatles, working bands played standards and they saved their rock material til the end of the night when they were really stretched out. It could be pretty lame.

Wayne Kramer

My house was full of music. My main memories are of the record player at home: it was all Beatles and Rolling Stones, and we danced around the living room; that started me off on instruments, and I've done nothing else ever since.

Steven Price

I used to love the Beatles and the Stones and I'd always want to hang out with them, even though they were about seven years older.

Peter Noone

Rolling Stones, Beatles, we gave them all the break they were looking for. All they needed was a good opening act, and we went out there and performed as well as we could... over 15,000 kids chanting.

Bobby Hatfield

I grew up with the Beatles and they are still to this day my top band played in my iTunes.

Greg Laswell

I was obsessed with the Beatles as a kid.

Sxip Shirey

The Beatles were perfect. There's just no other way to say it. They were the perfect band.

Danny Wood

I feel that Jane's is really a vibe and a time. It wasn't like we were the Beatles. We didn't have crafty pop songs where it sort of didn't matter who played them because they're just really great songs.

Eric Avery

The Beatles were no trouble... lots of girls. The Stones were black-jacketed guys, a rough crowd. A whole different scene between the Stones' black leather jackets and the Beatles' pretty-dressed girls with the ribbons in their hair, teenagers standing on the seats screaming, nothing broken.

Sid Bernstein

Then on to all the terrific american songwriters, from Tin Pan Alley to the Beatles, from Bob Dylan to Paul Simon. Whoever wrote and sang in the song form I have appreciated.

Tom Chapin

I don't remember 'Doctor Who' not being part of my life, and it became a part of growing up, along with The Beatles, National Health spectacles, and fog. And it runs deep. It's in my DNA.

Peter Capaldi

I have a very eclectic iPod. So I've got my cardio people - so it's anything from Beyonce to some Jay-Z to Janelle Monae, her song 'Tightrope,' that's a good cardio song. And then I've got Sting. I've got Mary J. Blige. I've got The Beatles. I've got Michael Jackson. I try to pick the songs that I personally love.

Michelle Obama

If it weren't for the Beatles, I would not be a musician.

Dave Grohl

The modern recording studio, with its well-trained engineers, 24-track machines and shiny new recording consoles, encourages the artist to get involved with sound. And there have always been artists who could make the equipment serve their needs in a highly personal way - I would single out the Beatles, Phil Spector, the Beach Boys and Thom Bell.

Jon Landau

Our influences are who we are. It's rare that anything is an absolutely pure vision; even Daniel Johnston sounds like the Beatles. And that's the problem with the bands I'm always asked about, the ones derivative of the early Seattle sound. They don't dilute their influences enough.

Eddie Vedder

You know how the Beatles broke off - they all did their solo projects and they came back together and they were even stronger!

Kelly Rowland

I never was a hippie! I went to India because so many friends like Mia Farrow and the Beatles were going there to discover truth. And so I went and trekked through India by myself, but instead of discovering truth, I wanted to join the Peace Corps.

Jane Fonda

I was a huge Beatles fan. We could talk about who I listened to growing up and what my sources were, but certainly the Beatles were a late, important resource for me, and I just took my guitar and a handful of songs, and I decided, well, I'll just go over and travel around Europe and see what comes of it.

James Taylor

Lennon was right. And we are bigger than Jesus. We will be as big as the Beatles, if not bigger.

Liam Gallagher

I've bought clothes based on record covers. Particularly from the formative music that turned me onto it in the first place when I was a kid, with the Beatles and the Small Faces. A lot of those Sixties soul artists were in really sharp sharkskin or mohair suits, and Motown artists looked amazing.

Paul Weller

I wrote 'Yellow Submarine' for the Beatles. I wrote the screenplay for 'The Games,' about the Olympic Games. I wrote 'Love Story,' both the novel and the screenplay. I wrote 'RPM' for Stanley Kramer. Plus, I wrote two scholarly books and a 400-page translation from the Latin, and I dated June Wilkinson!

Erich Segal

For me, the Beatles are proof of the existence of God.

Rick Rubin

You're not a baby boomer if you don't have a visceral recollection of a Kennedy and a King assassination, a Beatles breakup, a U.S. defeat in Vietnam, and a Watergate.

P. J. O'Rourke

We idolized the Beatles, except for those of us who idolized the Rolling Stones, who in those days still had many of their original teeth.

Dave Barry

I loved the Beatles when they turned up, and the Stones when they turned up, and never really stopped liking them.

Tom Stoppard

And it was a very, very fruitful and great relationship between the Stones and The Beatles. It was very, very friendly.

Keith Richards

At the end of the Beatles, I really was done in for the first time in my life. Until then, I really was a kind of cocky sod.

Paul McCartney

What the Beatles did was something incredible, it was more than what a band could do. We have to give them respect.

Yoko Ono

The true treasure lies within. It is the underlying theme of the songs we sing, the shows we watch and the books we read. It is woven into the Psalms of the Bible, the ballads of the Beatles and practically every Bollywood film ever made. What is that treasure? Love. Love is the nature of the Divine.

Radhanath Swami

We were pretty good mates until the Beatles started to split up and Yoko came into it. It was more like old army buddies splitting up on account of wedding bells.

Paul McCartney

I'm the worst on facts about me or facts about the Beatles.

Paul McCartney

I never went to rock concerts when I was a kid. I didn't see any rock & roll bands. I had posters on my wall. I had Beatles records.

Dave Grohl

From 1958 to 1964, that's real rock n' roll. Then the Beatles hit and everyone sounded like them.

Wolfman Jack

It's insane that, since the Beatles and Dylan, it's assumed that all musicians should do everything themselves. It's that ridiculous, teenage idea that when Mick Jagger sings, he's telling you something about his own life. It's so arrogant to think that people would want to know about it anyway!

Brian Eno

With every song that I write, I compare it to the Beatles. The thing is, they only got there before me. If I'd been born at the same time as John Lennon, I'd have been up there.

Noel Gallagher

The Beatles weren't like any other band. Everybody in the band sang, which is why you knew everybody in the band.

Gene Simmons

Well, the stuff that I liked growing up was AC/DC, Led Zeppelin, but I also liked the Beatles and guys like Cat Stevens and Elton John.

Dave Mustaine

When punk came along, I found my generation's music. I grew up listening to the Beatles and the Rolling Stones and Pink Floyd, 'cause that was what got played in the house. But when I first saw the Stranglers, I thought, 'This is it.'

Robert Smith

I had a guitar when I was 6 or 7, a plastic guitar with the Beatles' faces on it. It would be a collector's item now. It would fetch a hefty sum, I imagine.

Gary Oldman

I'm a huge music fan. I usually say that if I had been born with a musical inclination, it would've been great. The Beatles changed everything for me, and I wanted to be a journalist for 'Rolling Stone.' I'm a big music fan in a Cameron Crowe way, kind of in a spectator way.

Emma Stone

My favorite album would have to be something from The Beatles.

Liam Gallagher

Beethoven and Beatles, Mozart and Michael Jackson, Paganini and Prince - I like them all.

Vanessa Mae

I don't think anybody comes close to The Beatles, including Oasis.

Brian May

The Beatles, the Rolling Stones and Phil Spector. Those were my idols.

Brian Wilson

I did not become great by association of The Beatles! Beatles make Maharishi great? Pah! It is a waste of thought.

Maharishi Mahesh Yogi

The Beatles set the rules. And the rules were: now just because we have long hair doesn't mean that we're rebellious.

Davy Jones

I always loved LeAnn Rimes and especially Clint Black for his soulfulness. As I've gotten older, my influences have broadened - John Mayer, Michael Buble, Stevie Wonder, Keith Urban, Stevie Ray Vaughn, the Beatles - all of these artists have somehow been a part of my development as a songwriter.

Hunter Hayes

When I did get married and then had children, it was Beatles' songs I sang to them at night. As one of the youngest of 24 cousins, I had never held an infant or baby-sat. I didn't know any lullabies, so I sang Sam and Grace to sleep with 'I Will' and 'P.S. I Love You.'

Ann Hood

A song is a song. But there are some songs, ah, some songs are the greatest. The Beatles song 'Yesterday.' Listen to the lyrics.

Chuck Berry

Nervousness was never something I would ever associate with the Beatles ever. A Hard Day's Night was relatively unscathed by marijuana, but even then they were quite relaxed about it.

Richard Lester

I was inspired by the classic rock radio of the Seventies. They separated Chuck Berry and the Beatles from the Led Zeppelins and Bostons and Peter Framptons of the time. In many ways, classic rock became bigger than mainstream rock.

Chuck D

Ever since the Beatles, the concept of lovable mop tops, it's a bit of a fantasy, but it's a lovely idea that people make wonderful music and live a wonderful life being friends together. Sadly, life isn't quite like that.

Nick Mason

I do remember actually learning chords to Beatles songs. I thought they were great songwriters.

Mick Taylor

I think the Beatles are a lot of people's favorite band.

Miranda Cosgrove

The Beatles, Rolling Stones, Barbra Streisand, Bruce Springsteen, these are just some of the people who threatened to sue if we used their songs.

Colin Mochrie

The Beatles had some juice when it came to distortion, but Clapton was finally able to break through those early studio engineers' fear of overloading. He defined the sound that guitarists spend the rest of their lives trying to get.

Joe Perry

Growing up, I liked all the stuff that everyone else was listening to, like Motown, but the biggest group of all was The Beatles.

Eddie Murphy

You see Michelangelo and Picasso and you read literature. I had some innate inchoate yearning for that, but I never really saw where I would fit in. That's called art. And then something happened to pop music, which is that it became art under the hand of the Beatles, the Stones, and Bob Dylan and some other people.

David Chase

The Beatles just changed everything right across the board. They just had that right combination of clean-cut good looks - a cute band - but under that they had a real rock n' roll thing going on.

Joe Perry

I don't care about the word 'pop'. The Beatles were pop; it's just what's popular.

Jake Bugg

But in my imagination this whole thing developed and I started mixing up old folk songs with the Beatles beat and taking them down to Greenwich Village and playing them for the people there.

Roger McGuinn

Oh, I think country has changed tremendously. I think country has totally changed. Country music when I was a kid was Hank Williams. If you put Hank and Elvis together, there wasn't that musical difference. But as the Beatles showed up and the English invasion, I think country music got pretty far away from rock n' roll.

John Mellencamp

There are a lot of famous comedians from Liverpool, then obviously the Beatles, and the football club. That's what people in Liverpool are passionate about.

Ian Rush

The Beatles and The Stones were basically inspired by American Rhythm and Blues.

Mick Taylor

The Beatles are the most credible band in the history of music.

Ryan Tedder

There was always a lot of American music in England until, obviously when the Beatles came around, then there was a shift towards English music, but before then American music was the main thing.

John Deacon

Depth on different levels is so important to me. You look at a band like The Beatles, all their material has so much depth to it. And I want people to be able to run away with my melodies and get lost in them and take the lyrics and be able to relate to them.

Haley Reinhart

I suppose, counting back, if the Beatles had been influenced by music in the same length of time ago - you'd have to put that into better English for me, thank you - they would have been like a banjo orchestra. They would have been doing show tunes.

Jonny Greenwood

In the early '70s, coming out of the '60s, it was very hippy or it was very uniform, like The Beatles all wearing the same suit. Into the '70s, it became much more about a personal style. You had the glam period, which was a lot of fun, and then you went into punk.

John Varvatos

I had a really good time in New Orleans, although I had some very tragic times in Baton Rouge. Some guys beat me up and threw my horn away. 'Cause I had a beard, then, and long hair like the Beatles.

Ornette Coleman

I'm like, 'Would you be the person in the room that would boo when Dylan went electric? I know I wouldn't. Or are you the person that left The Beatles after 'She Loves You,' or 'Drive My Car?' You weren't on board for 'Revolution 9' or 'Day In The Life,' were you?'

Regina Spektor

So whenever I hear The Beatles I always feel I've got a lot in common with everybody else.

Robyn Hitchcock

I think comedy has a range, with multiple peaks in different areas. It's like trying to compare Beethoven and the Beatles. Sometimes I hear from people, 'I think you try too hard in your comedy.' And that's what I worry about.

Bo Burnham

The first time I heard The Beatles, I cried. It was 'Let it Be'.

James Durbin

From a very young age, music was very much in my house. I would sit with my mom, with the old LPs, listening to The Beatles and Carly Simon and Lionel Richie. The old LPs used to have the lyrics. From there, I would put on dance and music displays for my family, just to entertain them and make people laugh and smile.

Lara Pulver

I knew all this Beatles music. I knew the songs phonetically. It was like my whole experience of that music was out of focus, and somebody put the perfect glasses on me, and all of a sudden I could see everything.

Regina Spektor

You know, I was such a big Beatles fan, and when I'd buy a new album I'd invariably hate it the first time I heard it 'cause it was a mixture of absolute joy and absolute frustration. I couldn't grasp what they'd done, and I'd hate myself for that.

Andy Partridge

I grew up loving classic rock music - The Beatles, The Rolling Stones - and then one day I heard 'Baby One More Time' on the radio and I thought 'What is this?' I was eight and it changed my life.

Sara Paxton

I tried to emulate my favourite guitar players, the old bluesmen like Blind Willie McTell and Big Bill Broonzy. I used to sit by the record player and copy Chuck Berry and the Beatles. You can never copy someone completely, so you end up developing your own style.

Ronnie Wood

You're always frustrated, you don't have the chance to do a song on the album, like the Beatles did with Ringo and George, or like Led Zeppelin, where everybody was given a chance to contribute. There never is a chance with the Stones.

Bill Wyman

When I was a kid, I went through a lot of musical phases, and one was when I'd learn everything that The Beatles ever recorded. After I started drums, I fell in love with their music so much that I just wanted to learn everything.

Eric Carr

I thought my Beatles LPs sounded pretty good on a record player, but that was before I had heard a CD.

Alastair Wood

The Beatles' story is all of our stories. It is about how the youth culture emerged, the drug culture emerged, how politics rose to the fore as a universal debate. It's about rebellion, it's about the growth of the British entertainment system, the growth of the rock n' roll entertainment system.

Bob Spitz

I liked the Beatles because there was so much melody. Jimi Hendrix is still one of my heroes.

Robert Cray

I can't deal with the press; I hate all those Beatles questions.

Paul McCartney

She is the rock 'n' roll queen. Weirdly enough, that is one of the things her reign will be remembered for. Queen Elizabeth I, we remember Raleigh; Queen Elizabeth II it's gonna be the Beatles.

Paul McCartney

Growing up, I was inspired by The Beatles and Bob Dylan. Damian Rice was a huge influence for me musically.

Ed Sheeran

I think of talent as being God-given. I know that contradicts what a lot of people believe, but that's how I see it. I think the Beatles were meant to be, you know? So when I listen to Paul McCartney, I think, 'Here's the person that God gave the gift of allowing him to write 'Let It Be."

Brandon Flowers

The British invasion was the most important event of my life. I was in New Jersey and the night I saw the Beatles changed everything. I had seen Elvis before and he had done nothing for me, but these guys were in a band.

Steven Van Zandt

'The Beatles' did whatever they wanted. They were a collection of influences adapted to songs they wanted to write. George Harrison was instrumental in bringing in Indian music. Paul McCartney was a huge Little Richard fan. John Lennon was into minimalist aggressive rock.

Chris Cornell

My favorite artists have always been Elvis and The Beatles and they still are!

Johnny Ramone

Almost everything The Beatles did was great, and it's hard to improve on. They were our Bach. The way to get around it may be to keep it as simple as possible.

T Bone Burnett

I love Whitney Houston, Stevie Wonder, Brandi, Sade, Nat King Cole. I like the Beatles. I listen to a lot of that.

Leah LaBelle

The Beatles were a group made up of four very complex men, and my small hand could not have broken these men up.

Yoko Ono

The Beatles were basically a vocal band.

Keith Richards

People always say I write a lot of pop culture references. Can somebody please count the pop culture references in 'Firefly?' Because I don't know how to put this to you, but there was one. I referenced The Beatles in the pilot.

Joss Whedon

When I was growing up, the people who liked the Beatles, I didn't like, so I didn't pay attention to them.

Trent Reznor

They should invent some way to tape-record your dreams. I've written songs in my dreams that were Beatles songs. Then I'd wake up and they'd be gone.

Alice Cooper

If I were in the Beatles, I'd be a good George Harrison.

Noel Gallagher

The Beatles will never get back together and David Lee Roth will never again sing with Van Halen.

Alex Van Halen

My big love was the Beatles. I was more into music.

Gary Oldman

Sending greeting cards to aliens is hardly a new idea. In 2005, Craigslist solicited messages for broadcast to space by a transmitter in Florida, and in 2008, NASA beamed a Beatles song to the North Star (Polaris), on the assumption that any putative Polarians would appreciate the Fab Four's 1960s-genre compositions.

Seth Shostak

I am just a little tired of the Stones and the Beatles, and I don't care if I ever hear 'Louie Louie' ever again.

Wolfman Jack

My sister and I shared a bedroom our entire lives and I believe she discovered the Beatles when she was about 11 and I'm four years younger. So from the age of 7 until 17 we had nothing but Beatles paraphernalia in our room, even those little stuffed Beatles that went on stands that are dressed as the Sgt. Pepper band.

Christina Ricci

I was such a massive fan of all the '60s pop bands, but if I had to single out one band, it would definitely be The Beatles.

Paul Weller

I'll be honest. We copied everyone... the Beatles, the Bachelors. It was the only way people would even listen to you.

Maurice Gibb

Food culture is like listening to the Beatles - it's international, it's very positive, it's inventive and creative.

Alice Waters

I'm a huge Beatles fan, but I've only really gotten into them as an adult.

Serj Tankian

My mom listened to the Beatles and Elvis, a lot of different types of music.

Travis Barker

I didn't know much about him, and I wasn't a big country music fan. I listened to the Beatles and David Bowie, so I didn't know a lot about him.

Joaquin Phoenix

All you could do was to see them. We were backstage when the Beatles were on and you could just about hear a noise. It was just literally screaming.

Roger Daltrey

With all due respect to Mick Jagger, who is one of my idols, I think it's a mistake to leap around and sing at 53. When I started, there weren't any women I looked up to. It was Mick. I never saw anybody go on a stage and have that tongue-in-cheek attitude. It was all straight, including the Beatles. I love his attitude, hands on hips and lips out.

Grace Slick

I grew up a massive Beatles fan.

Dominic Monaghan

I was a huge Beatles fan. The Stones, Dylan. Later on, I got into Stevie Wonder, and Bill Withers - he's one of my heroes. Al Green, too.

Adam Levine

When I got into the Beatles, I must have only been about six or seven but old enough to take notice. We used to have an old radiogram which, for readers of a certain age, was like a big cabinet thing with a record player inside it.

Paul Weller

Men have made the world. And they've made a brilliant job of it. I love men. You know, men, you built Paris and you invented The Beatles, and, you know, and you've taught dogs to say 'sausages.' You know, I love your world. Thank you for it.

Caitlin Moran

I love the Beatles.

Eddie Murphy

I really consider myself fortunate to have been of age during the musical revolution that came in the form of the Beatles. People don't realize that previous to the Beatles, there really was no such thing as an album artist. People made singles. Then they would put a bunch of those singles together and call it an album. And that was it.

Todd Rundgren

It's nearly redundant to enumerate the reasons The Beatles are important. There are probably different reasons why The Beatles are important to a musician like myself and to the millions of Beatles fans who just enjoy listening to the music.

Todd Rundgren

As a performing group, the Beatles began by playing old rock favorites, for dancing, to tough audiences in Liverpool and Hamburg. When they began writing seriously, they discovered that they couldn't compose in the early American rock tradition.

Jon Landau

Haiti is my country. The same way the Beatles are received in England - that's how Wyclef Jean is received in Haiti, do you know what I mean?

Wyclef Jean

Do you realize that I have had five albums in the Top 30. Elvis and The Beatles have never done that. I had five singles in the Top 5, I mean, no one's ever done that.

Chubby Checker

The Beach Boys already had about four or five albums under our belt when these newcomers, The Beatles, took the U.S. by storm in early 1964.

Mike Love

I grew up listening to the Beatles and being an ardent Beatles fan when I was in third grade all the way to adulthood, and listening to all kinds of music that came to us either at the flea market or in our living rooms or on the 'Ed Sullivan' show - all these places we were influenced by.

Sandra Cisneros

From 1962 to 1965, the guitar became this icon of youth culture, thanks mostly to the Beatles.

Pat Metheny

The Beatles never sounded intimidated by their idols. They never interpreted old rock; they simply played it as well and as joyfully as they knew how. On 'Rock 'n' Roll,' John Lennon does nothing but interpret old rock.

Jon Landau

I'm wide open and will entertain anything anybody has to say, but if it's MTV and radio, well, they're great things, but can't be the only thing. I don't know that it would work even for the Beatles.

John Mellencamp

The Beach Boys have always been a part of the '60s spectrum, with The Beatles and that kind of thing. They were a part of the music business like everyone else. And they did quite well as a singing group, and I finished a lot of good records, and I'm very proud of them.

Brian Wilson

I don't know about friends, but what time I spent with The Beatles they were very courteous to me.

Peter Tork

Also, right at that particular time in the music business, because of people like the Beatles, people began owning their own publishing. I'll just say this really quickly - they used to divide the money for the music that was written in two, just equal halves.

Jackson Browne

I wanted to pay tribute to my musical influences: Buffalo Springfield, Lightfoot, the Beatles, the Hollies.

Dan Fogelberg

Paul McCartney and The Beatles in general are my idols. And I love Sting. I got to meet Sting. That was really cool. Dustin Hoffman is my favorite actor. Also, I think of Magic Johnson as an idol.

Nat Wolff

The muse of music isn't just from Greek mythology, but living in people like the Beatles, Chuck Berry, Anita Baker, Aretha Franklin.

Ernie Isley

The Rascals are something else. They're up there with the Beatles, and Stones and Byrds. That level of musicality. They have a real chemistry. It is like magic.

Steven Van Zandt

I was about twenty and the Beatles were meditating and I heard about it and they had a center in New York and I came to the center and I learned about it.

Ray Dalio

I actually didn't listen to the Beatles song 'Nowhere Man' when I was writing my book of the same name. What I listened to a lot was 'Abbey Road.' Its disjointedness and its readiness to confuse only to delight were inspiring to me.

Aleksandar Hemon

I don't listen to anybody's full record anymore and when I did, I don't think I listened to the whole record. I'm sorry, and I don't care who it is, if it's the Beatles, I can't listen to an hour and a half of anybody straight so I guess that's just my personal preference.

Tommy Lee

The Beatles were in a different stratosphere, a different planet to the rest of us. All I know is when I heard 'Love Me Do' on the radio, I remember walking down the street and knowing my life was going to be completely different now the Beatles were in it.

Justin Hayward

I was still listening to the Beatles until I came here, you know.

David Thewlis

My earliest memories as a child are listening to Beatles records, and they are a big part of how I've learned to write pop songs.

Christina Perri

My grandfather lived across the garden from us, and in his attic he had a lot of radios, appliances and inventions that he had made over 50 years, such as a keyboard called a clavioline, which can be heard on some Beatles songs - it was popular in the 60s. So we had all that at home.

Michel Gondry

I don't have an iPod. I don't get the whole iPod thing. Who has time to listen to that much music? If I had one, it would probably have Sinatra, Beatles, some '70s music, some '80s music, and that's it.

Scott Baio

I got this Christmas gift with the entire Beatles catalog. I had fun trying to duplicate what I was hearing on these records, only using the instruments I had at hand - an acoustic guitar, and that's all. It was endlessly amusing to me to try to imitate John Lennon and Paul McCartney's harmonies using the guitar.

M. Ward

When we were trying to get 'Jersey Boys' off the ground, I'd get, 'The Four Seasons? Who's going to care? There's the Beatles, there's the Rolling Stones.' But people know those stories. Here was a story no one knew.

Frankie Valli

Musicians of any era - whether it be The Beatles, the Rolling Stones, Rage Against the Machine, or, of course, Madonna - will inspire fashion. And we, in turn, will inspire them.

Renzo Rosso

The Beatles were raw musically, but I think they really had something.

Brenda Lee

The best pop music is the songs that a group of people can dance to, but you can also listen to in your bed and cry. That's something obviously that The Beatles started and... so having that darkness there opens another door.

Andrew Dost

If you look in my CD case, you'll see it's Pink Floyd, The Rolling Stones, The Beatles, now I can't think of anyone else, but all that stuff.

Michael Angarano

The Beatles were something everyone had in common; this was thirty years ago, there was Dr. Who and everybody knew who the Daleks were and there was The Beatles and everybody knew who George Harrison was.

Robyn Hitchcock

When you think about great teams, The Beatles and the Pythons immediately spring to mind. The Pythons were as much a part of their time as The Beatles.

Robyn Hitchcock

I'd always wanted to work in the studio and experiment with sounds. Things that I'm really influenced by and that I love are like The Beatles and Radiohead, and all those records by bands whose music is really involved.

Regina Spektor

My dad bought a Beatles tape when I was in fifth grade, and that was the first time I ever really - I mean I was into music, but that was the first time it really blew my mind. When I heard the 'Red Compilation,' which wasn't like a proper album, I thought, 'music was more than I had ever thought it was before.'

Andrew Dost

The Beatles did treat me as a member of the group. And that was a great honor, you know?

Billy Preston

The big turning point, really, was the Beatles' influence on American folk music, and then Roger took it to the next step, and then along came the Lovin' Spoonful and everybody else.

Barry McGuire

I respect my dad, and he's amazing. He's my hero. He's the Beatles, man - or one of them.

James McCartney

I have been influenced by many different artists at many different stages of my life. Starting out, it was people like Elton John, Billy Joel, Ben Folds, and Fiona Apple. As I got older I got deeper into the work of bands like the Beatles, artists like Sam Cooke, Ray Charles, Etta James, and Joni Mitchell.

Sara Bareilles

I think that one of the nice things about the Yellow Submarine movie is that it seems to be perennial. People enjoy watching from each generation. And it was like the Beatles themselves. You know the Beatles seem to find new audience each time another generation comes along.

George Martin

It's funny because if you ever ask anyone in England to try and do a Beatles accent, no one knows what they really sound like. If you ask anyone in America, they would try and give it a go. English people just know their songs.

Aaron Johnson

It's hard to live up to The Beatles. When Wings toured, they got slated. Even Dad found it hard living up to The Beatles. I started out playing under an alias because I wanted to start quietly.

James McCartney

The Beatles changed music forever. They took rock n' roll from a medium that was about cars and girls and gave it context, interesting chord changes and true musicianship.

Bob Spitz

The only people playing the roles of classic rock stars are hip-hop artists, now. Kanye's stage persona, and the way he approaches making albums, and the way he wants to be better than everyone else? That's reminiscent of Freddie Mercury. That's reminiscent of the Beatles.

Jack Antonoff

You can't beat The Beatles, you join 'em.

Peggy Lee

It's like this - these five members have been influenced of course by other groups, because that's where this generation's groups came from - an environment like the Beatles, the Rolling Stones, the Yardbirds, and The Who. People like that.

Alice Cooper

Many people, especially young people, have started listening to sitar since George Harrison, one of the Beatles, became my disciple.

Ravi Shankar

Even the Beatles lived their lives as a soap opera.

Chris Lowe

One day when I was like 9, I heard the Beatles on the radio, and I asked my dad who they were. He told me they were the best band in the world, and I became obsessed. He started giving me their albums in sequential order, and I listened to them - and only them - until I was probably in high school.

Lukas Haas

I was the first to promote The Beatles in the States, and Ed Sullivan called me first about them before he ever booked them on his television show.

Sid Bernstein

No one person could have broken up a band, especially one the size of the Beatles.

Yoko Ono

All I can say is, it's not very easy for a woman to be associated with The Beatles.

Yoko Ono

I just got into the Beatles a couple years ago, you know, I like it.

Ziggy Marley

I always kind of think if The Beatles were still around now, people would've lost interest quite a long time ago. Seven years of recording - it's there forever. I think not outstaying your welcome is a vital ingredient.

Martin Freeman

I can't actually believe how good 'The Sopranos' is. I genuinely am dumbfounded by it. It's like when you realize how good The Beatles are, and you think, 'How did they do that?'

Martin Freeman

The only movie I can watch on a loop, over and over, is 'Help', the Beatles movie. It's so funny and irreverent and great.

Emma Stone

I remember, when I was a kid, listening to the radio and hearing 'Big Bad John' by Jimmy Dean - and it just blew me away. I used to sit there and call the radio stations and request that song. And then the Beatles were obviously out already, but I really didn't know about the Beatles.

Nikki Sixx

The Beatles were a phenomenon, but they were also ordinary blokes like anyone else. I was lucky enough to see that side.

James Taylor

There's no outdoing The Beatles.

Brian Wilson

I grew up on a lot of early Beatles, DC5, Cream, Clapton, Page, Beck and Hendrix.

Eddie Van Halen

My inspirations include the Beatles - love, love, love them - Elton John, Carole King, and Stevie Wonder.

Gloria Estefan

Oasis are not just influenced by the Beatles; they actually take stuff. Then they get praised.

Lenny Kravitz

Every night I fell asleep to a different Beatles album. So I'm very familiar with the Beatles; Ringo was my favorite Beatle until I grew up and then changed. I made the switch over to George Harrison just in time to regain my cool.

Christina Ricci

And so we went away to play, and we'd come back to Liverpool. And while we were doing this - 'cuz we did it for two years. And then we'd go to Germany, and that's where I met the Beatles.

Ringo Starr

My sister discovered the Beatles when she was about 11 and I'm four years younger. So we had nothing but Beatles paraphernalia. Every night I fell asleep to a different Beatles album.

Christina Ricci

I could hum Beatles songs before I could talk - not very well, but sort of.

Taylor Momsen

I grew up in the day when the Beatles sold 1 million singles in a week. And all you've got to do now is sell about 10,000 singles and you're in the charts.

Phil Collins

I'm a giant Beatles fan.

Taylor Momsen

The Beatles did everything first, and they did it the best.

Taylor Momsen

I translated Beatles songs for my English class.

Christian Lacroix

While the Beatles always had George Martin around to clean up their act, the Rolling Stones had Andrew Loog Oldham to coarsen theirs.

Jon Landau

It's always been easy with Mark, he's a rock fan and we speak the same language. He's a big Beatles fan too. We worked a lot via CLI calls, though only meeting up once every couple of months.

Phil Collins

There's only one band that could ever even pretend to assume the mantle of what the Beatles did, who have been so pre-eminent and world-dominating that they could effect a paradigm shift in the culture, who have been willing to leverage their success into musical change, and that is U2 - regardless of what the result of that is.

Todd Rundgren

When I got out of the Nazz, I had it in my mind that simply to be eclectic was an important aspect of making music. It was something that I derived from The Beatles.

Todd Rundgren

When the Beatles first came out, you had to go to a certain amount of trouble to have long hair. You just couldn't have it immediately. Anything you can just go out and get - like platform shoes - is not going to inspire people as much as something they have to go through a little bit of hell to have.

Todd Rundgren

The Beatles production is often so 'perfect' that it sounds computerized. 'Sgt. Pepper' really does sound like it took four months to make.

Jon Landau

Even at al my mother's concerts, I had never seen people go crazy the way they did with the Beatles.

Lorna Luft

I grew up with Jilly and Tamsin driving Volvos. But I wasn't one of them... I always felt more comfortable with Cockney and working-class people. My heroes were the Beatles and people like Michael Caine.

Tracey Ullman

I think between The Beach Boys, The Beatles, The Rolling Stones and innumerable acts after that... rock music became a huge economic force.

Mike Love

I don't think there's anything anybody's doing that the Beatles didn't at least try at some point.

Joe Perry

I love that Euro-pop dance music, but with girl power. I also listen to Janis Joplin and Bob Dylan. I have a Beatles song tattooed on my foot. I'm all over the place.

Hilary Duff

I love the Beatles, and when I was very young, I had young parents, so Led Zeppelin and Janis Joplin and Jimi Hendrix and the Beatles constantly were big influences on my life.

Phil Anselmo

Hanson has rapid female fans, which I'm completely proud of, but a lot of fans are a contingent that have grown up with us really - our peers. There's younger fans. More and more guys are Hanson fans, musicians or kind of guys who were into a Beatles record.

Taylor Hanson

The Rolling Stones are constantly changing, but beneath the changes they remain the most formal of rock bands. Their successive releases have been continuous extensions of their approach, not radical redefinitions, as has so often been the case with the Beatles.

Jon Landau

The Stones were more dangerous than other bands of the Sixties. It looked like they had more fun than the Beatles - like they stayed up later.

Alex Lifeson

And I said, 'Why not? It's the truth! Why can't I say I'm a Beatles fan?' I used to get criticized for that.

Buck Owens

My music was typically continental - nothing like, say, The Beatles.

Giorgio Moroder

I like the Beatles. They're at the core of my musicality. And John Lennon's my spiritual father.

Esai Morales